Contents

The 10 Walks

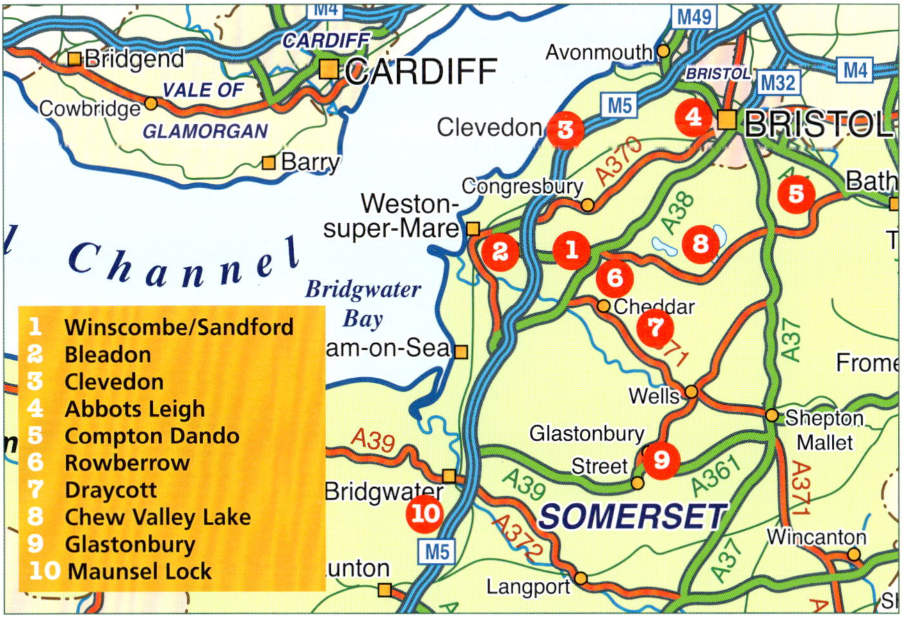

An Apple Alphabet

Ashmeads Kernel

An 18th century apple, from Gloucester. Intense flavour.

Gloucester Cross

Long Ashton Research Station Somerset, 1913. Eating apple.

Beauty of Bath

19th century, from Bailbrook near Bath. A distinctive eater.

Camelot

1930s apple from Yeovil. Cooks to a sharp fruity, golden purée.

Dabinett

Early 1900s apple. First found in a hedge in Middle Lambrook, Somerset. Cider apple.

Exeter Cross

Long Ashton Research Station Somerset, 1924. Eating apple.

Fair Maid of Taunton

Cider apple variety originating from that area of Somerset.

Harry Masters Jersey

Raised by Harry Masters, Yarlington, Somerset. 19th century. Cider apple.

Improved Dove

Cider apple variety from the Glastonbury area of Somerset in early 1900s.

Jersey Beauty

Eating apple from the Isle of Wight, 1926.

Kingston Black

Iconic cider apple from the Taunton area. Mid 18th century.

Long Tom

A cider apple variety peculiar to the Clevedon,Congresbury and Weston-super-Mare area.

EST. 1904

THATCHERS
Family Walks

10 circular family activity walks in Somerset with an apple theme

by SUE GEARING & LES DAVIES

Welcome

Born and bred in the Mendips, walking is in my blood. We're so lucky to live in this part of the country, in my mind there is nowhere better. With the beauty of the Levels and their amazing wildlife, to the intrigue of the hills with their vast history, it's there for us all to share.

I'm looking forward to following these walks, compiled by our good friends Sue Gearing and Les Davies, with my family and friends.

The walks are on our doorstep, and all take in the very special Somerset atmosphere.

I hope you get as much pleasure from them as I know we will.

Martin Thatcher
Managing Director
Thatchers Cider

What is so special about this book?

This book is for families to explore the countryside together. It's a walking book with a difference.

Here are ten short circular walks in Somerset. They are explorations with fun activities such as making a compass in a puddle, building a small shelter and finding the age of a tree. All these can be found in the back of the book.

Also look out for our ***Spot Checks***, one in each walk. Some are easy to find, while others may not be. Keep your eyes open!

We have also included a series of ***Did you Know?*** nuggets of information.

We hope you enjoy this book, because we enjoyed writing it.

Sue Gearing and Les Davies

Morgan Sweet
Another icon! Cider apple that can also be eaten. From 18th century Somerset.

Northwood
Cider apple from Devon, a pure sweet apple from the 1700s.

Old Rock Pippin
From the Glastonbury area, early 1900s.

Pomeroy of Somerset
Aromatic with a distinctive flavour, a Somerset apple from the 1850s.

Queen
From Essex. Raised by a farmer in 1858, a great baking apple.

Royal Somerset
Dual purpose apple for cider or cooking from the mid 1800s.

Stoke Red
Cider apple found growing in Rodney Stoke, Somerset in 1926.

Tom Putt
The 'cottagers apple' from the early 1800s. Rev'd Tom Putt was from Trent in Dorset.

Upton Pyne
Raised in Devon in the early 1900s. Cooks to a purée with pineapple like flavour.

Valise Apple
Also known as 'Redskins' and originated in North Somerset. Eater/cooker/cider.

White Jersey
Cider apple originating in late 1800s. Somerset.

Xavier de Bavay
A late season eating apple from Tasmania; a long way from Somerset!

Yarlington Mill
Somerset cider variety. Said to have been found growing at the Mill in Yarlington.

Zabergau Renette
From Germany, which is also a long way from Somerset!

Winscombe - Sandford Hill - Sandford - Strawberry Line - Winscombe

7.3km (4.5 miles) • Allow about 2.5 hours walking time
OS Explorer Map 141 • Cheddar Gorge & Mendip Hills West
Grid Ref: 420 576

Sandford has been the home of Thatchers Cider since 1904, and is in the centre of this varied, interesting and beautiful circle from Winscombe. Stop at Thatchers' renovated Railway Inn and then head back, past the old Sandford Station along the Strawberry Line railway path. En route, pass the former Sandford quarry and forge, with evidence of where Italian prisoners of war worked. At the end enjoy Winscombe Millennium Green at the old station and look at the time line.

Walking is on a mixture of footpaths and tracks which should be mainly dry under foot, with some stiles. In season enjoy bluebells in Sandford woods. There is one steady but modest climb up Sandford Hill. It is a good walk for dogs too.

A Activities to enjoy:

• Magical sticky stones • Make a mini shelter • Shapes in the trees

PARKING

In Winscombe. There are free car parks at the side and behind the Woodborough Inn in the centre of the village.

START

Turn up the side of the Woodborough Inn on Hillyfields Way, a narrow lane. Continue on it as it becomes a footpath. Ignore side turns.

1. FIELD

Come into a field and fork left, looking ahead to wooded Sandford Hill. Cross a stile and concrete footbridge and old stone stile and keep on across the field. After another stile aim straight ahead down the length of the field. A stone stile at the end leads onto Shipham Lane.

2. LANE

Follow it left. Just before a bend, notice one of Thatchers' cider apple orchards on the left. At the bend, turn right towards 'Uplands' going down a drive where a noisy and friendly donkey may greet you. At the junction with a house ahead, turn left and shortly, at the entrance to a small campsite, turn up right climbing gently. Continue ahead up to a stile towards the woods.

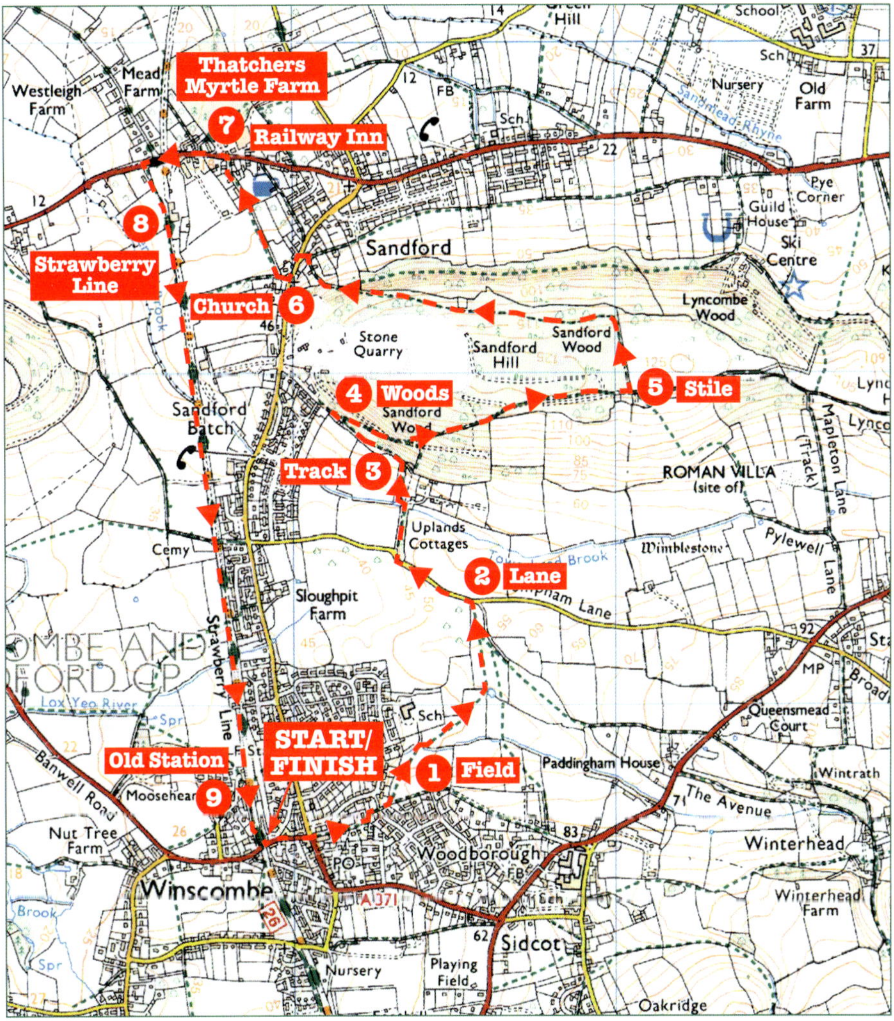

3. TRACK

Cross and turn left on the track. Soon pass a roofless breeze block wall – the remains of a urinal used by Italian prisoners of war.

During the last war they came up from Wells where they were in a camp and worked on the quarry in Sandford Woods. Near here also was a canteen, since demolished.

Continue on past Rose Cottage and soon take the small path ahead on the right past the remains of the forge, linked to the work in the old quarry. Go past and up steps into Sandford Woods.

4. WOODS

Reach a track at the top which used to be an old rail line to the quarry, ferrying explosives from the store in the woods. Turn right. Pass a bench and viewpoint looking across Winscombe to Crook Peak, the only pointed hill on Mendip. Pass the old quarry awarded to the parish in 1798 so they could dig out stone to rebuild local roads. This 'Award land' is now being managed for public access and nature conservation by a group of local volunteers.

SPOT CHECK

Can you find this object?

At the end of the path – a former railway track – carry on, to where another track joins from the right. At a fork, take the left track and follow this up through the woods to the end.

Before the barrier at the end, go left over a stile and follow the path with the quarry fence on your left.

A ***Why not try sticky stones along here?***

It is a beautiful area of mixed woodland where further on you will notice a number of quite large holes, known as Bell Pits, the remains of Ochre mining.

Ochre was used as a paint pigment throughout history. The remains of collapsed 'bell pits' can still be seen. This was an ancient method of mining where the mineral was dug out from a shaft and lifted to the surface in buckets by a windlass. As

the mining underground widened out, it formed an underground 'Bell', which due to the roof being unsupported was either abandoned when it became unsafe, or collapsed.

A ***The woods are a good place to make a small shelter of sticks for a very small animal.***

Further on pass warning signs for the old Sandford Quarry behind the fencing.

Sandford Quarry dates back to the mid 1800s and provided the stone for such building projects as Avonmouth Docks and Temple Meads Station. Prior to this the Parish used its own land alongside the quarry to provide stone to repair its own roads from 1799. It is now a Nature Reserve.

A ***Through the woods, look out for shapes you may see in the trees, on both living and dead trees which could look like a monster, a face, or an animal perhaps.***

Drop down and eventually reach a stile onto a small path which continues downhill and comes out at houses on the edge of Sandford. Go out onto the road which leads from Sandford to Winscombe. Cross with care and turn left for about half a minute.

5. CHURCH

Opposite the Methodist Church, turn right on the public footpath through the church car park by the scout hut. Then go right, following a grassy swathe alongside another of Thatchers' orchards.

Did You Know? *Thatchers Cider Managing Director Martin Thatcher planted his first apple tree in 1973 at the age of 5.*

A ***Why not try making a grass whistle?***

At the end, join a short residential drive which takes you to the main road in Sandford.

6. THATCHERS MYRTLE FARM

Opposite are Thatchers' offices, and the completely renovated and extended Railway Inn is a couple of minutes walk on the right, where you can enjoy refreshment. Thatchers' shop is just past it.

Retrace your steps back to where you joined the main road opposite Thatchers' offices and continue on a little further. Pass St Monica's residential care development built on the site of the old Sandford quarry and by the old Sandford station. A little further on, turn left and this leads onto the Strawberry Line walk and cycle path.

7. STRAWBERRY LINE

At weekends in season you can go up left to see the old station, the platform, a train and the Railway Heritage Museum, beautifully run by volunteers and well worth a visit. There is also a buffet in the old station for drinks and snacks.

The Strawberry Line dates back to 1864 when the Somerset & Dorset and Bristol &

Exeter Railway Companies joined forces to link the main line at Yatton to Wells and then onwards through Shepton Mallet to the south coast. The name comes from the railway line's importance in sending the early strawberries from Cheddar valley villages up to the London markets. But the line was also valuable to passengers, and vital for quarrying, agriculture and general goods.

Since the last train in 1963, community efforts have opened up the line from Yatton to Cheddar as a cycle and walkway. The ambitious aim now is to open up the remaining sections, from Clevedon on the coast to the market town of Shepton Mallet.

Continue on the Strawberry Line for about 1.8k (just over a mile) going through Cheddar Valley Nature Reserve (there's an information board) and all the way to Old Station Green.

8. OLD STATION

Pass the old mounting for a crane and then reach the Millennium Green Sculpture.

*It looks like a pair of railway lines snaking into the distance. Some say that the 'SS' stands for **'Strawberry Special'**, the name given to the regular passenger service along the line.*

Go and read the information board so you can work out the lay-out of the old station. Stand in the old ticket office, etc. Imagine you are waiting for a train in about 1908. What clothes did you wear? How much was the ticket?

Along the old platform is a fascinating time line made up of paving slabs along the edge of the old platform. It traces our history from the Birth of Christ to the start of this century and has metal plaques showing different events in history. How many years does each slab represent?

Bear down left to the road in Winscombe. (there are toilets on the right) and turn left past shops back to the Woodborough Inn. But first look at the rail bridge, which has a story.

It was prepared for demolition after the line had been closed, and in fact the one at Sandford was demolished. However, it is said that the demolition company went bankrupt before this bridge could be brought down. An interesting story that leaves this bridge still intact. Had the Sandford bridge remained it would have been far too low for Thatchers delivery vehicles to go under, and the story of the company, possibly somewhat different!

***Did you know?** This bridge was designed by a former Sidcot School pupil. Read the plaque by the bridge to find out more.*

Facilities

Sandford Station
Railway Heritage Centre
Open April 1- Oct 31, Sat & Sun, 11 am-4pm, drinks and snacks.
Tel: 01934 843868.

The Railway Inn Sandford
Tel: 01934 611518.
www.therailwayinn.com

Bleadon - Hellenge Hill - Bleadon Hill - Shiplate Slait - River Axe - Bleadon

8.17 km (5.07 miles) • Allow about 2 hours walking time
OS Explorer Map 153 • Cheddar, Weston-super-Mare & Bleadon Hill
Grid Ref: 340 568

A beautiful circle from Bleadon, western Mendip, round the sheltered bowl below Shiplate Slait where Thatchers have a huge orchard. It will be a picture if you can come in apple blossom time. From the village our route goes up through a nature reserve to the Roman Road which runs along the top. Here is a good all-round viewpoint and then it's across on tracks to the open plateau. Below is the track down hill with good views across Somerset to the south.

The walk has a good contrast at the end – a route along the River Axe. In Bleadon is the popular Queen's Arms pub, serving Thatchers cider. It is one of the longer routes in the book and has an uphill section, followed later by a downhill.

A Activities to enjoy:

• Compass in a puddle • Magical sticky stones • Cloud shapes

PARKING

Park in the free village car park just south of the church in the centre of Bleadon on Coronation Road. There are the Coronation Halls here, toilets and a children's playground and picnic area. There is also an interesting information board about the history of Bleadon and the discovery of Bleadon Man, a replica of which is in the Coronation Hall. It also notes the martyrdom of a former Rector of Bleadon who defied Henry VIII and was hung, drawn and quartered in 1514 in London.

START

Turn up left on the village road, Coronation Road. Up ahead, in view, is the Queen's Arms which you may like to visit now or later. We don't pass it. Go over the road to the old cross and church with its very typical Somerset tower, visible for miles around. Go through the churchyard and out the other side, and then turn up left to reach Shiplate Road and turn right. Follow it for a few minutes and look for a public footpath sign on a power pole by the roadside. Follow it up a drive on the left, starting the ascent of Hellenge Hill.

1. HELLENGE HILL

Go through onto the open area of Hellenge Hill maintained by Avon Wildlife Trust. It is an SSSI, a Site of Special Scientific Interest.

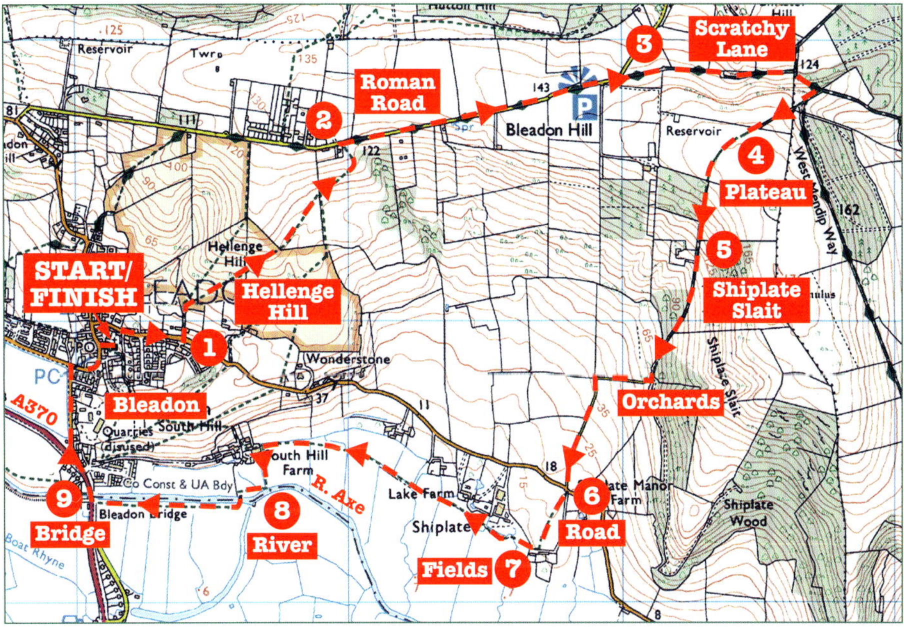

The hill's chalky grassland has a number of rare plants such as honeywort and Somerset hair-grass which are only found on the hot southern scarp of Mendip. Look out also for green-winged orchids, carline thistle and autumn lady's tresses. It is a good wildlife habitat and don't be surprised on a sunny day to see adders basking on the slopes.

Soon reach a footpath marker post. Bear up right following the West Mendip Way (WMW). Stay on the left track at a fork, still the WMW. Go through a kissing gate and now just maintain direction, climbing, following the WMW through fields.

You get good views down over Somerset and Brent Knoll and the curve of the River Axe below. As you progress start to see ahead, down right, the vast Thatchers Cider orchard taking advantage of the warmth and shelter of this south facing slope.

Your route takes you up towards a house, buildings and fence. Go round to the right of the raised plot up to a Bristol Gate, a field gate with a pedestrian gate included in it.

Did you know? *The Bristol Gate – pictured left – is so named because the original idea came from two Avon Council footpath wardens in Bristol.*

2. ROMAN ROAD

Turn right on the Roman Road. This is actually a little to the south of the original Roman route across Mendip bringing lead and other minerals from Charterhouse to the port of Bleadon down on the River Axe which was navigable at that point. Continue all the way to a parking and open grassy area on the left which is a great viewpoint looking across as far as Clevedon. Continue on a little further.

3. SCRATCHY LANE

At the bend, go straight on along a footpath, known as Scratchy Lane, and still the route of the WMW.

A ***Along here, after rain, you may be able to try out Compass in a Puddle. It would also be suitable to try some Trail Art.***

Turn right at the first T-junction, climbing again on a stony track. At the top, turn right following the WMW a little further, in the Loxton direction, still ascending.

A ***This could be a good place to try sticky stones.***

4. TRACK

The WMW then leaves and goes left but you continue straight on up a track until

you go through a gate ahead into the open grassy plateau.

Here is one of the finest views on the Mendip Hills looking over Weston-super-Mare, and Steep Holm – the last and most westerly hill of Mendip – the Severn Estuary and Wales.

A ***This is a great place for spotting shapes in clouds.***

Head across enjoying the 'top of the world' feeling, if the wind doesn't bowl you over! A gate on the far side takes you onto a small path to the left of trees and this drops down Shiplate Slait.

5. SHIPLATE SLAIT

Did you know? *'Shiplate' means 'sheep path' and goes back at least as early as the 10th century.*

You may still see sheep grazing here, which is appropriate as this was described as one of the finest sheep slaits (pastures) in England at the end of the 18th century.

Join a tarmac lane/drive and look across to Thatchers' orchards, and in the field above the orchards see a rectangle of cultivation which is John Thatcher's vineyard! Continue down going now between orchards to the Loxton-Bleadon road at the foot.

These orchards were planted with the aid of a Geographical Positioning Satellite (GPS). There are over 100 acres of new trees including *Dabinett*, *Tremletts Bitter* and *Lizzie*.

Did you know? *The apple variety Lizzie was named after Liz Copas who worked with the late Ray Williams (Willy) at Long Ashton Research Station. They bred a range of new cider apples now being grown by Thatchers.*

6. ROAD

Cross towards Shiplate Fishery and take the marked footpath through a kissing gate on the right. Follow the left fence down and then along the foot and in the second corner go through a gate and along the hedge and over a footbridge.

7. FIELDS

Go into a field and follow the rhyne – pronounced *'reen'*, a drainage ditch or canal. Continue through fields and gates in the same direction, on the flat, passing one or two houses on the right and a farm in the hamlet of Shiplate. Reach a stony drive heading towards a farm straight on.

Immediately on reaching the farm, turn back and follow the fence on the right, heading straight to the farm. Continue down the field with the farm on your right

Go right through a Bristol Gate in the corner and along with the River Axe on your left. Then through a gate into another field.

SPOT CHECK

Can you find this object?

8. PARFITTS BRIDGE

Soon reach a bridge over the Axe – Parfitts Bridge. Cross and turn right, now following the river on your right. Continue all the way to a gate and the A370 road.

9. BLEADON BRIDGE

Turn right, cross Bleadon Bridge, and view the large tide gates and sluice.

The Axe rises 20 miles away in Wookey Hole and before the construction of the doors here in 1802, the river was navigable for coal vessels and small craft as far as Cheddar. It also had important fisheries but for a long time these were ruined by poisoned water from lead works at Charterhouse and by chemical refuse from paper mills. Today, it is once again favoured by anglers and the water height monitored by the Environment Agency.

Continue on along the road, and through a parking area at the side, and cross the side road, Bleadon Mill. Just past a garage, take the road on the right to Bleadon – a fairly quiet route following a rhyne on the left.

10. CORONATION ROAD

At the T-junction turn right on Coronation Road, soon coming to the car park.

FACILITIES

Queen's Arms, Bleadon
Tel: 01934 812080.
Open daily.

Clevedon (Walton St Mary) - Coast path - Castle Hill - Clevedon

4.7km (2.16 miles) • Allow about 1.25 hours walking time
OS Explorer Map 154 • Bristol West & Portishead
Grid Ref: 340 568

A short morning or afternoon circle along the beautiful coast path between Clevedon and Portishead with great views across to Wales.

From the coast, the walk turns inland and circles back down a reasonably quiet lane and then up through woodland and along a high ridge. Try and choose dry conditions and a clear sunny day to enjoy it to the full. Young children will need to be kept under control along the coast path. There are only a couple of stiles. Find plenty of good picnic spots on the way but there are no refreshment places. However, there is a great choice back in Clevedon.

The origins of cider are lost somewhere within the passage of time, but one thing would have had a bearing on its arrival in this country and that is the sea. As an island nation for the past 10,000 years, all of our culture would have been imported, and that includes agriculture. Trading along this coast line could well have brought the idea of a fermented apple drink from Spain or the Middle East. Today, several apple varieties owe their existence to this area of North Somerset: Backwell Red, Congresbury Beauty and Court de Wick are just a few.

A Activities to enjoy:

• Magical sticky stones • Make a mini shelter • Make a grass whistle

PARKING

In Walton St Mary on the eastern side of Clevedon by St Mary's church (maybe in Channel Road) or in the parking lay-by at the start of Bay Road.

START

From the church go down the road and turn right into Bay Road where there is an alternative parking place in the lay-by. Soon turn down steps onto the coastal footpath and turn right.

The views across the estuary to Wales and the bridges can be spectacular on a clear day. The tidal range at Clevedon is the second highest in the world with a rise of

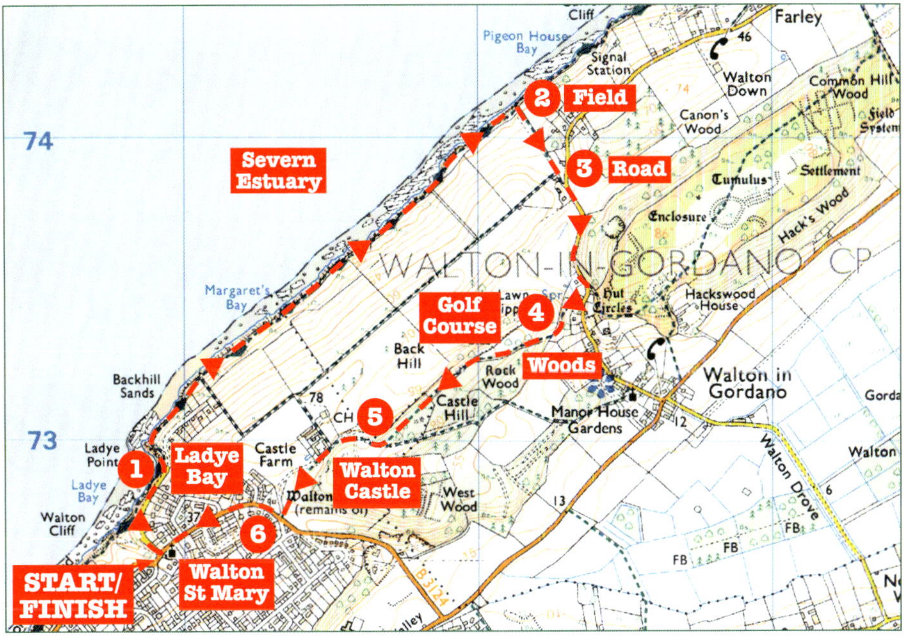

over 14.32m (47 feet) from low water on Spring Tides. The tides are very strong. Don't be tempted to go into the water. The shore is a mixture of pebbled beaches and low rocky cliffs and has been designated as the Clevedon Shore Geological Site of Special Scientific Interest. Notice the different rock formations and rock 'balconies' as you go along.

Soon reach a path which takes you down to Ladye Bay.

1. LADYE BAY

A ***This could be a fun place to build a small stone shelter using beach pebbles and sticks.***

Follow the undulating coast path on and come to open land rising on the right. In Spring there is usually a good display of bluebells.

Soon you can get a good view of the second Severn Crossing and maybe even the original one, as you go on further.

2. FIELD

After about 2.89km (1.8 miles) along the coast, cross right over a stile into a field following the footpath sign.

Climb up the left side, getting even wider views behind as you go. This would be a great spot for a picnic on a sunny day. Leave the field, go along a short track and over another stile onto the road.

A ***This would be a great place to make a grass whistle.***

3. ROAD

This leads up from Walton in Gordano and there is a pavement or verge along the edge, so turn down right for a few minutes. Just past Springhead Cottage, take the footpath on the right which follows the stream.

As you turn up steps on the left look to the right and see a hole under the wall by the stream. This allows the stream water to escape at times of flooding.

4. WOODS

Climb up into the woods. The path is quite good underfoot.

A ***This might be a good place to have a go at Trail Art.***

It is quite a long climb but eventually reach a ridge on Castle Hill, looking down right over the golf course and beyond it to the Severn Estuary.

5. GOLF COURSE

Go through a wicket gate with a sign warning you to watch out for golfers. Walk along the right side of the golf course and see ahead Walton Castle which is now privately owned and available for special occasions and for holidays.

This 17th century hunting lodge atop the wooded hill is one of the landmarks of Clevedon. It was for many years a ruin, but has been restored with meticulous care to resemble the original.

Reach a track on the right which drops downhill. Go down through a gate, and on along the tarmac drive.

At a slight bend, at Horseshoe Cottage, fork left across the golf course on a stony track passing a golf tee.

A little further on, fork right on the marked path and come down to the end of the golf club drive through a wicket gate.

6. WALTON ST MARY

Go down to the road and turn right in Walton St Mary all the way back to the church and the start of the walk.

SPOT CHECK

Can you find this object?

Abbots Leigh - Abbots Pool - Ashton Court - Leigh Woods - Abbots Leigh

7.24 k (4.5miles) • Allow about 3 hours walking time
OS Explorer Map • 155 Bristol & Bath
Grid Ref: 543 738

You don't have to scratch the surface of the landscape around here very much, to find the cider apple connections below. Long Ashton Research Station was for many years a world leader in apple and cider research. Now sadly gone, its legacy remains in the apple varieties discovered there. Newer varieties such as Prince William and Hastings,(being grown by Thatchers today) have joined the older varieties such as Ashton Brown Jersey that were discovered at the Research Station. Abbots Leigh is also the home of the original orchard planted by Redvers Coate, for Coates Cider in the early 1950s. Ashton Brown Jersey, and Sandford Jersey are still to be found in this orchard, whose rows dip down the slope to the road leading to Abbots Pool.

As well as a great variety of apples that this area has produced, it has also come up with this walk of contrasts. It takes in the wooded beauty spot of Abbots Pool where the monks used to fish, and then high open Ashton Court estate with great views, a café, miniature railway and then the Nature Reserve of Leigh Woods, before following the Monarch's Way back. It's easy walking with no real hills. In Abbots Leigh is the fine George Inn with good food – and Thatchers Cider.

Bluebells, and other wild flowers can be enjoyed in season and you can spot water birds on Abbots Pool. In the Autumn plenty of sweet chestnuts can be found too.

A Activities to enjoy:

• Fly a kite • Guess the age of a tree • Make and sail a boat
• Make an apple flapjack for a picnic by Abbots Pool

PARKING

In Abbots Leigh village, either in Manor Road near the George, or opposite in Church Lane. Or you could start half way round in North Road, Leigh Woods, near the entrance to the woodland area of Leigh Woods and follow directions from there. The George would then be en route.

The word 'Leigh' comes from Old English 'Leah' being a clearing in a wooded settlement. Abbots Leigh was the special retreat of the Abbot of St Augustine's Abbey, Bristol, where Bristol Cathedral now is.

START

Walk down Manor Road at the side of The George pub.

The pub is one of the oldest buildings in the village and was originally a church house and stable, providing a venue for church ales! During the mid 1750s, churchwardens let the place as a public house with rent being used for the church.

Soon pass on your right the old Priory built in 1831 in Gothic style.

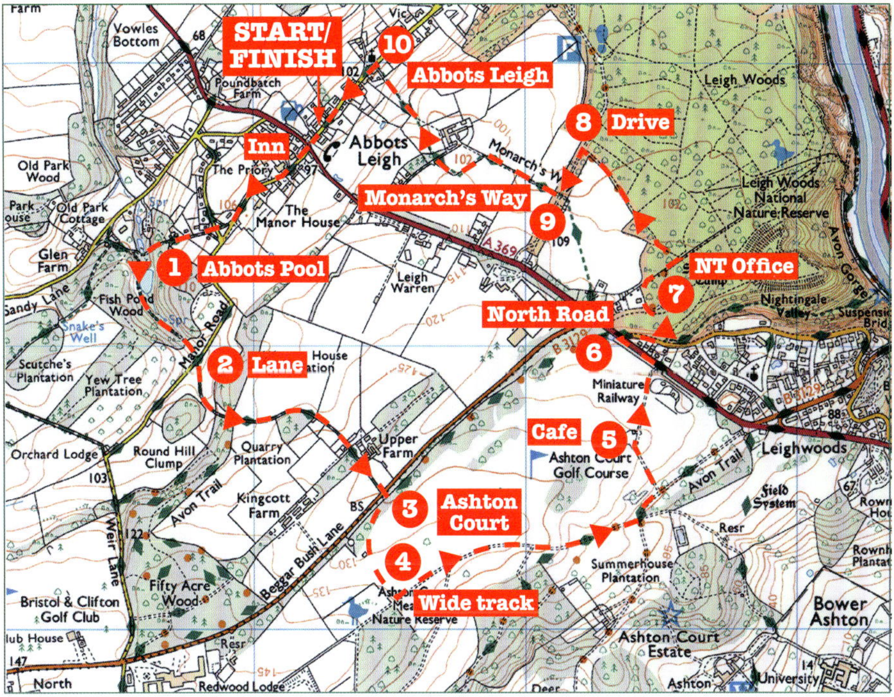

This was once the home of the Fry family of chocolate fame and here in the conservatory, Janet Fry bred silk worms to provide silk for her passion for church embroidery. It is now subdivided into several homes.

Pass on your left a former manor house, now a care home.

Continue all the way to Grangewood House on the right and take the footpath straight on along the wall. Cross a drive and join a stony track. Maintain direction dropping down. Go through a kissing gate with an information board about the Pool.

1. ABBOTS POOL

The three ponds would have been created by damming the brook, probably for the Abbot as a fishpond, stocking fresh fish for the pot. Walter Wills, the tobacco magnate, owned the property from 1915-1945 and landscaped the pond by raising the level of the dam. The Wills family also constructed the cascades below the dam. An Island (on stilts) and a cave were created. This beauty spot is now under the care of North Somerset Council.

Legend had it that when Henry VIII shut down the monastery in 1538, the monks' treasure, rather than being surrendered to the crown, was brought here and thrown into the Abbots Pool. But no-one has succeeded in finding it!

Keep on downhill following the wall and fence on your right and down steps to a bridge over one of the ponds. Don't cross. Go left this side of the lower pond and then go up steps to the higher and main pond. See the cave grotto left. Cross the dam.

A ***This would be a great place to make and sail a leaf or twig boat.***

It is an ideal picnic spot too – great to eat your apple flapjack here!

Turn left along the other side of the pool, coming out at the end through a barrier by a parking area. Continue on between apple orchards. Notice a concrete structure at the front of the orchard right. This was built as a loading bay for sacks of apples.

These are on the site of the original ones planted for Redvers Coate of Coates Cider in the mid 1950s. It was a revolutionary style at the time – planting the trees in hedgerows, which once again is back in fashion.

2. LANE

Cross a lane and carry on up a track, climbing gently, and then flattening out. Eventually reach the main road. Cross with care and go left for 50-60 metres and then right through an opening in the wall into Ashton Court estate.

3. ASHTON COURT

Ashton Court Estate, once the gracious home of the Smyth family, covers 850 acres of woods and grasslands designed by Humphry Repton and now a major leisure area for Bristol. It dates back to before the 11th century and is a great venue for weddings and other events.

Look out for major annual events such as the International Balloon Fiesta in August and Bristol International Festival of Kites and Air Creations in September.

Go in a few yards and then right on the bridleway (white topped posts) which runs alongside the road and then bears away left.

The edge of the golf course here is a great spot to see a wide variety of wild flowers. Go across the end of the golf course. Pass a gate into the marked Ashton Court Meadow nature reserve on your right – worth a visit if you are interested in wild flowers such as wild carrot, yellow-wort and field scabious.

Turn left on a track which comes back down to the wide crossing track to continue from **4. WIDE TRACK**, or leaving out the

We think this looks just like a Tree Monster! Can you spot it?

nature reserve, continue ahead until you reach a wide crossing track.

4. WIDE TRACK

Turn left and follow this all the way across the high open land with great views over Bristol and to your right up on the ridge is Dundry village and church.

A ***Fly a kite.***

Start to drop down and see ahead on the right a walled garden.

A ***There are some good trees along here for you to try guessing their age.***

Pass a stone dew pond, a drinking pool for animals. At a crossing of tracks, go left joining the main drive. Reach a barrier and another junction and turn left up the hill to the golf club and café.

5. CAFÉ

This is a good place to stop for a drink or snack.

Turn right on the stony path which reaches the Miniature Railway *(see above)*, open on selected weekends in season and run by the Bristol Society of Model Engineers. Just past the railway go towards the main road and then turn left under the trees. Shortly, look out for a gap on the right taking you onto the main road. Cross with care and turn left for about a minute.

6. NORTH ROAD

Turn right down North Road (an alternative starting place). After about a minute cross and go left through a kissing gate into Leigh Woods. Go straight on. After about another minute, fork up left and come to an open area. Turn left along the edge and go through a kissing gate between house and bungalow.

✓ SPOT CHECK

Can you find this carved crocodile in the woods?

7. NT OFFICE

Come to a National Trust office. Go past it and turn right on a stony track by Post 41. Pass a wonderful carved wooden crocodile. *(see above)* somewhat hidden on the left under a tree.

Just before a gate and fence ahead, turn left through a wall opening and straight ahead on the path in the woodland.

8. DRIVE

This takes you all the way to the main tree lined drive where you go left.

At a signpost, turn right on the Monarch's Way.

9. MONARCH'S WAY

Go through a gate and ahead on a grassy track across the field. In the corner follow the edge left (or usage shows that many walkers cut the corner off) and keep going until you reach the next corner with a gate.

Go on to reach a crossing tarmac track and go straight over and shortly come into a field with Abbots Leigh up ahead. Maintain direction now heading for the church going down and up the undulating fields, finally coming up through a play and picnic area to the end of the road in Abbots Leigh.

10. ABBOTS LEIGH

Turn left, pass the church on your right – a 15th century Perpendicular Gothic building – restored and partially rebuilt in 1847-48 after a fire, and get a magnificent view across to Avonmouth and beyond.

Continue along Church Road to the George pub or to where you parked.

FACILITIES

The George, Abbots Leigh
Tel: 01275 37698

Compton Dando - Woollard - Lord's Wood - Compton Dando

7.6km (4.7 miles) • Allow about 2.5 hours walking time
OS Explorer 155 • Bristol & Bath
Grid Ref: 646 645

A glorious North Somerset circle – ideal for Spring – that follows the Two Rivers Walk for some of the way and goes alongside the River Chew. It starts from Compton Dando and explores the undulating countryside and woodland. There are many different wild flowers including two glorious bluebell woods and different trees to identify. Although there are several hills, none is too long or strenuous. Walking is on tracks and good footpaths. En route are several ideal picnic spots and at the end you can enjoy a glass or food at the Compton Inn. This walk has kissing gates and no stiles except for one very high ladder stile (which can be avoided) so the whole circuit should be ideal for man and dog.

This walk is almost equal distant between Bristol and Bath (13km/8 miles away) where Thatchers sponsor Bath Rugby Club. There are still the remnants of farm orchards around the walk, the fruit from which is made into local cider or sold for processing. The apple variety 'Beauty of Bath' is a well known eating apple that has roots in this part of Somerset.

Activities to enjoy:

- ***Leaf whistle • Look for a four leaf clover***
- ***Leaf rubbing • Have a picnic***
- ***Make a mini shelter of sticks suitable for a small animal***

START

In Compton Dando in the Chew Valley, about 4.8km (3 miles) south of Keynsham and two miles east of Pensford. Park in the village centre near the Compton Inn, or if you plan to eat there afterwards the landlord may allow you to park there, so ask.

From the Compton, cross the road and take Church Lane opposite. Go through the gate by the old lychgate, joining the Two Rivers Walk. Go down the right side of the church and out down steps. Head across right to the old mill, mentioned in the Domesday Survey and take the footpath at the side which brings you to the picturesque old

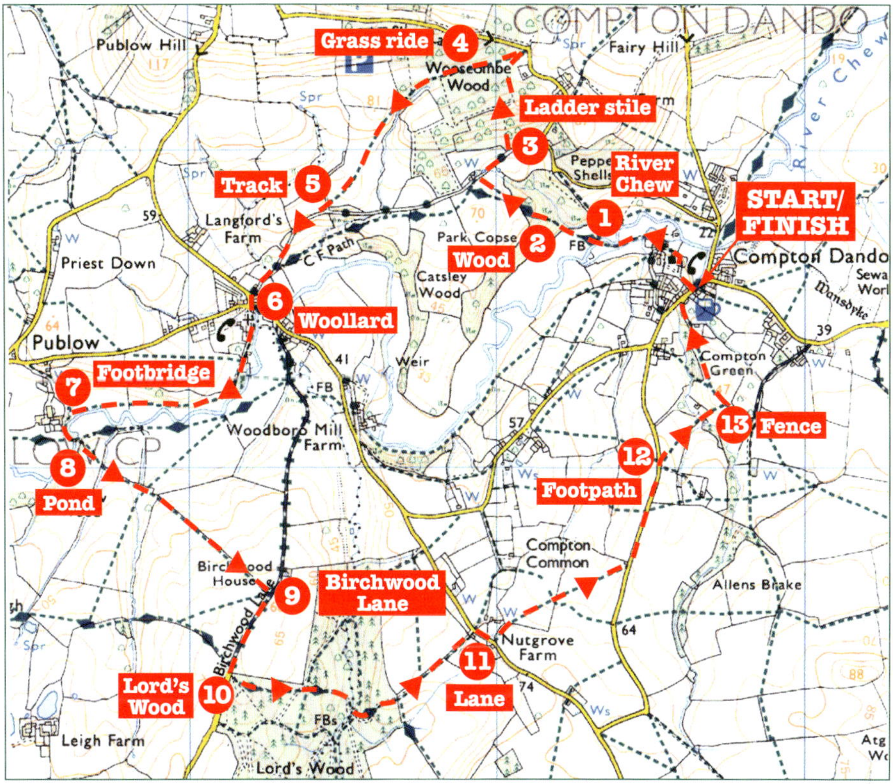

mill pond, complete with ducks. Turn left along the pond edge, and go on through a gate and along the grassy path which soon brings you close to the River Chew on your right.

1. RIVER CHEW

Cross the footbridge and take the footpath which goes ahead slightly left across the field to a gate into woodland.

2. WOODS

Enter the wood, at its best in spring with wild garlic, wood anemones and many bluebells. The main path ahead is the one you want which climbs steeply up to a gate at the top of the wood. In the field, bear across right heading to the right of a house.

Cross onto a track and turn right. At the end join a tarmac lane. Go on a few metres.

3. LADDER STILE

There is a choice of routes here – one using the ladder stile and footpaths, and the other up the quiet lane.

For the footpath route: Go up over the high ladder stile tucked into the hedge, left, on a permissive path. Check that the stile is not in a dangerous state. Follow the path up through a mixed wood plantation,climbing. There are great views at the top. Turn right on the wide grass swathe for a few metres and then left crossing over to

another, smaller woodland path which drops down, crosses a grassy ride, and on through Wooscombe Wood. It comes out on another wide grass ride where you turn left joining the other route.

Alternative: If you want to avoid the ladder stile, stay on the lane. Turn left at a junction and follow the high banked lane uphill and then level out. Bend round and take the first footpath on the left through a kissing gate onto a wide grassy ride.

4. GRASS RIDE

Continue on down the ride.

A ***Tree identification and leaf rubbing. There is a wide variety of trees on each side of the ride. Take one or two of the leaves with good veins back home and do a rubbing.***

? ***Did you know?*** *The wood of aspen trees (and there are several along here), were traditionally used for making matchsticks. It is a short grained wood, easy to work, yet porous enough to absorb chemicals, but has to be strong enough to resist breaking or bending when struck. Not too much to ask!*

Go over to the left of the ride. Ignore a grassy track turning left and instead take the path ahead of you which takes you into the woodland.

Go through, using a kissing gate and footbridge en route and another gate at the end into a field.

Here are beautiful views across to the south over Somerset – a good place for a rest and a picnic in the sunshine.

A ***Looking for a four leaf clover is always worth a go. They do exist, and are said to bring good luck to those who find them. Also a good place to try out making a grass whistle.***

Go straight on down, through a gate and on, as before to the bottom right corner and a kissing gate onto a crossing track.

5. TRACK

Turn right. This leads down and bends right into the hamlet of Woollard.

6. WOOLLARD

Turn left and shortly, at the T-junction with the village road, cross straight over into Mill Lane following the River Chew on your left. Pass a converted chapel right and pretty riverside homes. At the end, take the footpath to the right of a cottage, leading into a field and continue on. Another gate, and go right following the line of the Chew down on your left. Continue along, either going up onto the bank at the top of the field, or staying close to the water. Whichever you choose, come into another field and carry on following the river, still on your left.

7. FOOTBRIDGE

After several minutes, just before a farm, arrive at a large very beautiful sturdy oak footbridge over the Chew – quite a labour of love. Cross this and then bear ahead across, slightly right to meet the right fence. Ignore a stile and gate on the right. Stay in the field alongside a farm track and climb.

8. POND

Go through another gate and reach a pond, a good picnic spot. Ignore the gate left. Stay on the right of the fence and continue on up through a wooden kissing gate into a field.

Follow the left edge of the field, climbing steadily, with good views behind.

At the end come onto a drive/track – Birchwood Lane.

9. BIRCHWOOD LANE

Follow it right.

10. LORD'S WOOD

After a few minutes, turn left into Lord's Wood, rejoining the Three Rivers Walk. This is another beautiful bluebell woodland.

A ***Make a small shelter of sticks and decorate it as you like with leaves and or moss and stones.***

Go more or less straight over a crossing track and on down a smaller woodland path into a valley with a pond and along the edge. Drop left down steps to a crossing of tracks. Head straight over and climb uphill. As you get onto the flat, you may notice a wild apple tree on the left.

SPOT CHECK

Can you find this object?

This apple tree is a seedling that has grown from a pip. All our apple varieties have been discovered this way, and the very best were grown on to give us the huge number of named apples we have today.

Did you know? *A lot of cider apples are high in tannin and low in acid. These qualities are said to have been inherited from the trees that resulted in cross pollination (several hundred years ago) between the domestic apple, introduced into Britain from Asia Minor, and the wild crab apple here.*

Continue on to a gate into a field. Walk ahead along the top of the field.

11. LANE

It brings you to a lane. Turn right for about a minute. Opposite a house look carefully on the left for a footpath going up steps into a field. Then it's left along the edge.

Don't miss a gate soon on the left to a plantation. Bear across diagonally right.

After another gate into the next field, go diagonally left up to the top left corner and through a wooden kissing gate (depending on crops you could go round the left edge although it is longer). Come through the gate onto a lane. Now go left along here for a few minutes on the flat across this open high land. Continue to the second footpath right and turn into a field.

12. FOOTPATH

Take the left footpath which drops down across the field. Head for the far power post in a line of three. It has a yellow tab and behind it is the kissing gate you

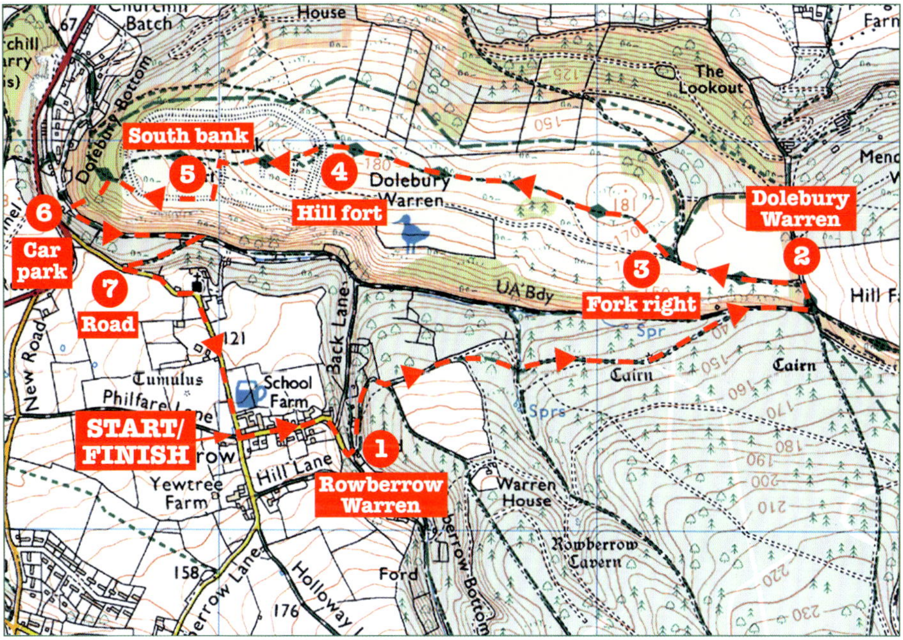

the 19th century looking for work at the mineries at Charterhouse.

The great social reformer Hannah More, and her sister Patty, were involved with the local community. Although warned to stay away as it was a somewhat 'hostile' environment, that didn't stop them!

1. ROWBERROW WARREN

Turn left at the foot and through a barrier to enter Rowberrow Warren. This was once heathland like Black Down, and was planted up as a forest after the Second World War. The return to heathland can be seen where the trees have been cut down.

A ***Why not collect a leaf or two with good veins and have a go at a leaf rubbing at home and leaf identification.***

Follow the track uphill into the forest, where quite a lot of clearance work has been taking place. Notice the ruins of old cottages, once used by miners in the area, in their quest for calamine.

SPOT CHECK

Can you find this object?

Mendip calamine was judged to be the best in the country. This was sent to Bristol for the brass making industry. Mining for calamine in this area dates back to about 1665. Later calamine was smelted to produce zinc, also used for Bristol brass making. By 1779, Bristol brass was in great demand, and Shipham and Rowberrrow became the centre of the zinc mining industry. At this time it was reported that the entire population of the two villages (around 700 people) was engaged in mining, with over a 100 mines in Shipham alone, many of them 'in the street, in the yards and some in the very houses'.

By the start of the 19th century, the industry was in decline. In 1839 it was reported that only one or two mines were working, and that by 1853, all operations had stopped. In the 1860s and 1870s some of the Shipham miners were employed in the leadworks at Charterhouse and they trudged there daily up the Slaggers Path.

At a junction at the top bear left. There is a field on your right as you go along, and soon begin to drop down. Take the second

turning left, still in the forest but with views, light and space after some of the clearance work. Bear left on the track, as a grassy track continues ahead, and drop downhill.

At the bottom, go left a metre or so to a T-junction with a stony track and turn right. It rises and leads you all the way to another T-junction. Go left here.

2. DOLEBURY WARREN

After about 80m reach a sign on the left for Dolebury Warren and cross the stile into National Trust land, managed by Avon Wildlife Trust. Stay on the track parallel with the left fence and now head up this beautiful open grassland – an area that often has a great variety of wild flowers. Cross a stile by a gate ahead of you and carry on up.

3. FORK RIGHT

As you approach woodland, reach a post with a yellow Limestone Link marker and fork right.

The Limestone Link is about 58km long and links two limestone areas – the Cotswolds and the Mendip Hills.

At the next waymark post, turn left which takes you through woodland. Once out in the open, carry on up, and soon cross another stile by a gate.

4. HILL FORT

Reach the outer (East) bank and opening of Dolebury hillfort.

This is a later entrance, as the original gateway into the hill fort lies at the western end. As it was the weakest side, it has a double protective bank.

Go through into the Iron Age hillfort.

Later it was used by the Romans and

Saxons. There is no evidence that it was ever attacked. This is one of the most beautiful viewpoints on Mendip, looking across to Crook Peak, the only pointed hill on Mendip and across the Bristol Channel. Let your imagination run free as you sit here and soak up the view.

Years ago you may have watched Roman war galleys putting in at the mouth of the River Axe, or may have watched a sea fight that drove the pirates of Brittany over to Wales.

Soon reach a bumpy stony mound – the remains of a warrener's house.

Did you know? *Rabbit was a very important part of the diet centuries ago so it was an important job to look after the rabbit warren. The rabbits were for the Lord of the Manor only, hence the need for a warrener to keep watch and keep everyone else out! The warrener's house had three stories: the lower for storage, the middle for living and the top as a look-out. More than 20 traps were set up and there were also long 'pillow mounds' to encourage the rabbits to burrow and breed within the hill fort.*

A ***Up here you could try playing Jacks, or play sticky stones.***

Keep straight on down the centre, and another track will join from the left. Go on this for a few metres, more or less in the same direction, and about now head across left over the rough grass to the southern bank of the hillfort which you can clearly see.

5. SOUTH BANK

Notice how steep the side is. It would have been difficult to attack the fort from here, and the ditch banks would have been faced with stone to make life even more difficult for an attacker. This grassy warm south facing slope is a favourite basking spot for adders. From here you look out across Rowberrow Manor and church.

Turn right along the bank – either the upper one, or the lower ledge, keeping the steep slope plunging down left. In the south west corner, find steps and a small path to go down and then on down many steps. It is steep, so watch your footing.

6. CAR PARK

At the foot, cross a stile into a muddy parking area. Go left through a gate and along the track, seriously eroded by use and water over the years. Keep on for a few minutes, passing a corrugated iron hut on the right on the other side of the fence. Soon after, turn right on a footpath – a small stony path which climbs up to the road leading into Rowberrow.

7. ROAD

Turn left and a few minutes later reach 14th century Rowberrow church. Carry on round the bend and look across right into a field and see a grassy round mound.

This is the site of a Bronze Age barrow approximately 20m (66ft) in diameter, which was excavated in 1813, and is believed to have given the village its name as Rowbarrow meaning 'rough hill' or 'barrow'.

Follow the road on and soon reach the Swan.

FACILITIES

The Swan, Rowberrow
tel: 01934 852371

Draycott - Draycott Sleights - Rodney Stoke - Draycott

7km (4.3 miles) • Allow about 2.5 hours walking time
OS Explorer Map 141 • Cheddar Gorge & Mendip Hills West
Grid Ref: 473 505

This is the area that gave rise to the cider apple variety Stoke Red. A bitter sharp apple discovered in the village of Rodney Stoke in the 1920s, it probably came originally from Wedmore. This is an area of warm south facing slopes with deep rich soil that gave rise to a thriving strawberry industry that sent its famous Cheddar Valley strawberries to Covent Garden in London via what has become known as the 'Strawberry Line'. Find out what a Thankful Village is, enjoy magnificent views, wild flowers, birds and butterflies in a National Nature Reserve. This winning walk starts from Draycott with a fairly steep and long climb up the southern edge of Mendip.

Then it heads along the side offering great views across to Glastonbury Tor, Nyland Hill, Crook Peak, Brent Knoll and beyond. Drop down through Stoke Woods National Nature Reserve, a great place for bluebells, and then comes a memorable stop on a well sited seat looking across to Glastonbury Tor. Go through Rodney Stoke with an ancient church and a Thankful Village memorial stained glass window. Pass alongside raised beds of strawberries, and if you wish, visit a popular village pub in Draycott before following the route of the old Strawberry Line back. There's a Cider and Ale barn, serving snacks, at the start.

A Activities to enjoy:

Flying a kite • Make a mini shelter • Leaf rubbing

PARKING

At Draycott's village hall with a good car park. Tuck yourself well out of the way. The hall is down Latches Lane, off the A371 Cheddar to Wells road.

Head back up the entrance drive, cross the main road and walk straight up the lane opposite towards the Mendip ridge.

1. WEST MENDIP WAY

Then continue on going over a junction onto the West Mendip Way footpath through a gate. Go straight up two fields. Shortly past farm barns, go left over a stone stile and then bear up right on a grassy track uphill (not close to the wall). Reach a gate with stone stile alongside. Once over, go up the valley a short way to a big boulder. Turn up right on the track which soon bends left and continues on up.

2. DEWPOND

Pass a dewpond and cross a stile by a gate.

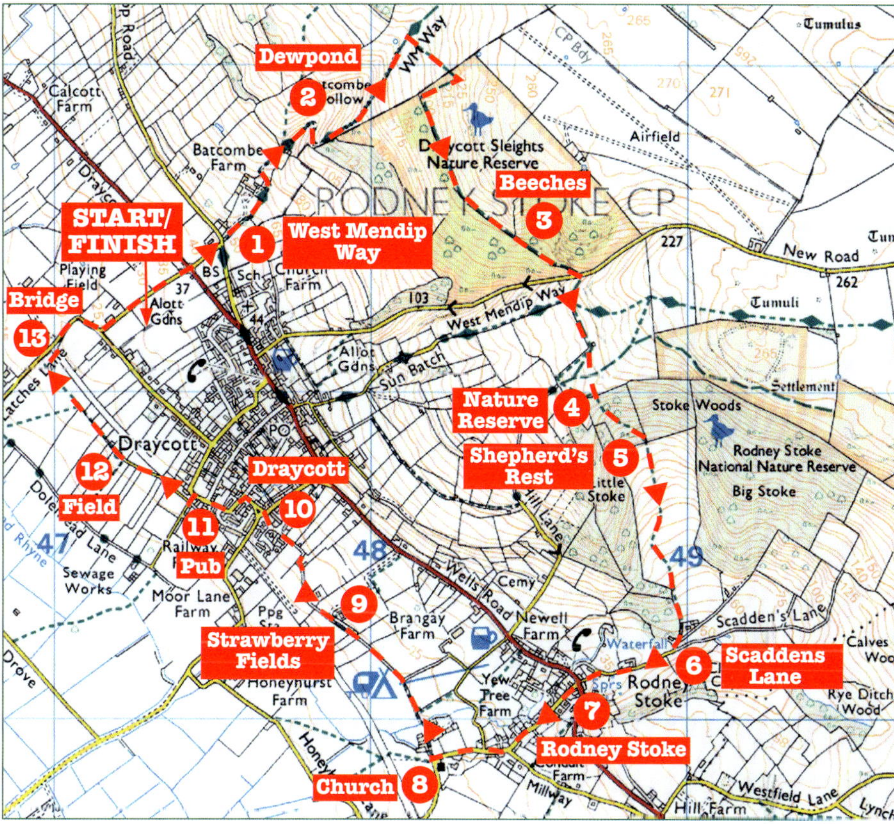

Continue on up the track until near the top where you reach a crossing track – the West Mendip Way. Follow this right and it takes you across and through a gate on the far side. Immediately turn down right downhill on a wide grassy track.

Go left through a gate to pick up a good track alongside the hill with really great views over the Levels, to Glastonbury and beyond.

A ***Could be good for flying a kite.***

Many wildflowers grow here, including cowslips, green winged orchids, autumn ladies tresses, kidney and horse-shoe vetch. You may also spot butterflies – the Chalkhill Blue, Brown Arqus, Grayling or the Dark Green Fritillary.

3. BEECHES

Continue on and come under a line of magnificent beeches, planted as a shelter belt. Continue on to go through a gate onto the crossing lane.

Here is a Somerset Wildlife Trust information board about Draycott Sleights. Go over the stile opposite joining the Butcombe Trail and Samaritan Way. Ignore the track right. Just continue straight ahead on to the bumpy grass ahead and soon the track is parallel down on the right. Notice the large lumps of 'pudding stone' along here.

These date back to the Jurassic period some 200 million years ago. Storms on what was then a much higher Mendip, washed masses of rock and debris from the mountain side to create an almost concrete like material that has become known as 'Draycott stone'. It was found to be ideal for gate posts and stile slabs which still exist today.

The West Mendip Way track heads up left but you just maintain direction. Go past a derelict barn and on to trees on the far side.

4. NATURE RESERVE

Cross a rod and stone stile to enter Rodney Stoke National Nature Reserve, an area of ancient ash and small leaf lime. Follow the main track downhill which is quite steep and could be muddy.

A ***It could be good for picking a leaf for leaf rubbing at home and leaf identification.***

A ***Mini shelter building.***

5. SHEPHERD'S REST

At the bottom a stile leads to a grassy field and one of the most beautiful views on

A beautiful view early on in the walk

Mendip looking down the valley, usually grazed by sheep, and across to Glastonbury. Here is a well sited seat, Shepherd's Rest, to enjoy views and the sun. Go down the valley and aim for the bottom right corner to the right of the house below. Cross a stile, and a path leads to Scadden's Lane.

6. SCADDEN'S LANE

Go right on the lane, soon passing Scadden's Farm and at a left bend, leave the lane. Go straight on along a path following the stream and passing a small waterfall. Pass a phone box and the old village pound where there is a Thankful Village plaque.

What is a Thankful Village? *There are thought to be about nine in Somerset, where everyone returned from World War I.*

7. RODNEY STOKE

At the main road in Rodney Stoke, cross

and turn left, shortly go right down Stoke Street. Follow this all the way down past village cottages to the 12th century church of St Leonard's.

8. CHURCH

Notice the ancient yew in the churchyard. Inside in the church are some beautiful bench ends carved by young men of the parish, and have a look also at the stained glass Thankful Village memorial window.

Turn right opposite the church down the railed track past a farmhouse. Pass a very ancient building on the right .

This is part of Manor Farm House – attached to the farm buildings – and is a small Elizabethan building called a gatehouse with mullion windows. There are the remains of a doorway flanked by columns set on high plinths. Such a building as this must have been important, as the stone work around the doorway is not what would be expected for a 'utilitarian' building. Perhaps much of this stone came from the derelict Glastonbury Abbey after King Henry's displeasure led to its demise!

✓ SPOT CHECK

What is this object?

Carry on through a gate into a field ahead along the right edge. Ignore a first footpath on the right and go on a little more to cross a marked stile right onto a lane.

SPOT CHECK

Can you find this object?

9. STRAWBERRY FIELDS

Turn left. Along here pass commercial strawberry growing with lines of strawberries on raised beds. Later, the lane turns into a track. Just continue all the way to reach the edge of Draycott.

10. DRAYCOTT

Maintain direction. Cross Bay Lane and go on towards Cheddar passing a walled triangle of overgrown vegetation left – could it be an old animal pound?

Stay on the lane and then bend left and right into Station Road with the old railway running along on the left.

11. PUB

Reach the Strawberry Special pub, serving lunch on Wednesday and bar snacks on Saturday and Sunday. Opposite is the old station.

This was once the route of the busy Great Western Railway line bringing early strawberries and vegetables from this area to markets in Bristol and beyond. The pub was named after the train of the same name. The line was closed under the Beeching axe in 1963.

Go left in Milking Lane and then immediately right on Hardmead Lane – the route of the old railway. Notice a 1908 small round Great Western Railway iron plaque on the left. Go through a gate at the end, passing stables and straight on along the path until you come into a field.

12. FIELD

Just head across passing Nyland Hill over left. Cross a stile onto a lane and right over the old railway bridge.

13. BRIDGE

Follow the lane along and round, passing Draycott Hall, to the main road.

Here on the left is a popular Cider and Ale barn open all day.

Then turn back right up the hall drive.

FACILITIES

The Strawberry Special, Draycott
Tel: 01934 742177
Full roast lunch Wednesday, and toasted sandwiches on Saturday and Sunday.
Closed other days at lunchtime.

Cider and Ale Barn, Draycott
Tel: 01934 741837
Open daily from 12 noon.

Chew Valley Lake - Knowle Hill - Chew Magna - River Chew - Chew Valley Lake

6.8km (4.2 miles) • Allow about 3 hours walking time
OS Explorer Map 154 • Bristol West & Portishead
Grid Ref: 573 814

A pleasant Chew Valley circle full of interest and contrast. It starts along the lake edge and then it's up and over Knowle Hill for fine views and across through the pretty countryside to Chew Magna where the Bishop of Bath and Wells used to have his palace. For the return, cross an old packhorse bridge and follow the River Chew back through fields. There is a café and toilets at the start and refreshment options in Chew Magna. Take your binoculars to enjoy the bird life to the full. It is a good dog walk although care must be taken to keep control. This walk has several Bristol Gates and kissing gates which have taken over from the old traditional stile.

A Activities to enjoy:

• Bird spotting • Calculate the age of a tree • Stick racing
• Make and sail your own boat

PARKING

At Chew Valley Lake Picnic Area and car park on the north side of the lake just east of Chew Stoke. Parking fee is £1.80 all day (2014), but free from October to end March. There is a café and restaurant here, Salt & Malt.

It's hard to imagine just how the landscape of this valley was before the arrival of the lake. It supported four mills, contained several farmsteads, each of which had its own orchard for cider production, and for supplying the house with fruit. Trees were in abundance, mainly English Elm, which has now gone forever from our landscape. It was a very tranquil valley.

The lake was built in the early 1950s by flooding the valley of the River Chew, and was opened by Queen Elizabeth II in 1956. It provides much of the drinking water for the city of Bristol and surrounding area, taking the water from the Mendip Hills. The lake is an important site for wildlife and has been dedicated as a Site of Special Scientific

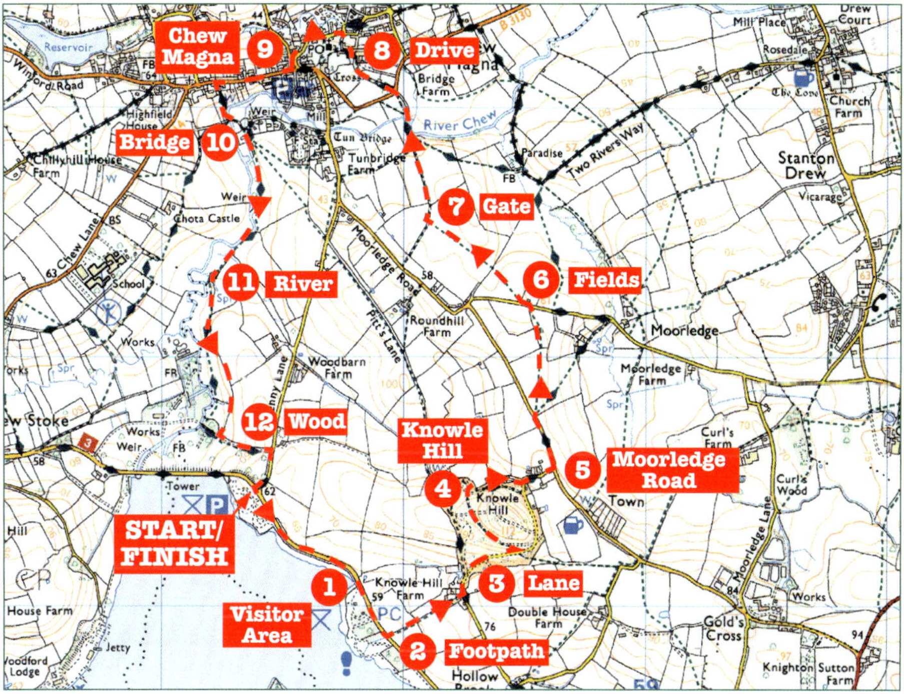

Interest (SSSI) and a Special Protection Area (SPA). It is a national centre for bird watching, with over 260 species recorded, including some unusual sightings. The lake has indigenous and migrant water birds throughout the year, and two nature trails have been created. The flora and fauna provide habitats for some less common plants and insects.

1. START

Turn back up towards the entrance and then go right on the stony path which takes you along the lake edge with the water on your right. There is a good view over Denny Island.

A ***If you have binoculars with you it is a good idea to see how many different kinds of water birds you can spot.***

1. VISITOR AREA

Continue to the next parking and visitor area. Turn up the entrance drive and reach the road.

Cross with care and turn right along the edge for a few metres.

2. FOOTPATH

Go left onto a footpath through a metal kissing gate and up the left edge of two fields. There was a flock of geese feeding in the stubble when we came in late August.

? ***Did you know?*** *A kissing gate is called such because the gate had to touch, or 'kiss' the upright post of the frame in which it was set.*

At the top by houses go out left through a small gate and then up right by the houses and out onto a lane.

3. LANE

Opposite is an information board about Knowle Hill. Go left on the lane. Ignore a footpath on the left and further on, about 100m past a drive to a house on the right, look for a path going up left onto the hill. (If you go on a little more you will see the footpath sign in the trees on the right.)

4. KNOWLE HILL

Follow the path uphill through the bracken, with good views over the lake unfolding as you go. Ignore side paths. Notice some of the new tree planting that has taken place on the hill. Continue on the flat, with the lake over on your left, all the way to a T-junction of paths on the hill. Turn right, and after a few more metres turn up right again. Stay on the main path. Pass a left fork which we will take on the way down, but for now carry on up a little further to the small open area at the top of Knowle Hill where the views over the lake and all round are remarkable. The two paths that lead down from here are not always very clear or easy, so the best way is to go back down for a short distance to the fork in the path and go down it right. This is kept mown and is an easy way off the hill.

Reach a tarmac drive and turn right. At a T-junction, turn left on the lane and follow this down and round to a junction with Moorledge Road.

5. MOORLEDGE ROAD

Turn left. If you want the popular Pony and Trap pub it is a couple of minutes along the road to the right – a small detour.

Carry on along the road for two or three minutes, after turning left.

6. FIELDS

Shortly, on the right go through a kissing gate up steps and take the path which goes diagonally left across the field staying up. So for the next section you get very pleasant views across the countryside. Go just to the right of the power pole in the field and on across to a kissing gate a few metres up from the far right corner. Once through, follow the bendy left edge, passing a small farm quarry hidden under the trees. In the corner, by a house go down through a gate and turn left on the lane.

A few metres on go up steps on the right and through another metal kissing gate. In the field go diagonally cutting off the left corner. The field was full of a nitrogen rich clover crop when we came. Go through a metal kissing gate on the far side and down into another, much larger field. Go straight across.

7. GATE

On the far side is a Bristol Gate ahead. Go through and along the grassy track along the field edge. Stay with this and come down, joining another path, the **Two Rivers Way**, and come alongside the River Chew down on your right under trees. Go through a Bristol Gate and along a path to another gate into a field.

Walk straight across, parallel with the right edge and go out onto the B3130.

8. DRIVE

Cross with care and go up the drive to Chew Court opposite under a magnificent avenue of limes.

A ***This avenue of limes would be a good place to check on the age of the trees by measuring the circumference of the tree at chest height.***

A figure of 25mm for each year of growth will give you an estimate of the tree's age. What was happening when these trees were planted?

Pass some staddle stones. Corn ricks were built on these to allow air flow below and more importantly to keep the vermin out, as they couldn't climb around the tops.

Reach the entrance to the Court.

This magnificent house, now a private home, was once the palace of Gisa, Bishop of Bath and Wells. It was visited by Henry III in 1250. Very little remains of the original palace but Chew Court is a surviving part.

Go right along the wall and then bend round and go ahead through a rather unusual metal stile and up steps into the churchyard of St Andrew's, Chew Magna.

The church dates dates from the 12th century and its beautiful 15th century pinnacled sandstone tower is more than 36m high. Notice that St Andrew's is still guarded by grotesque gargoyles round the tower and nave roof to keep evil spirits away. Of interest in the churchyard, is an early 19th century limestone round-topped stone which bears the inscription to William Fowler "shot by an Highwayman on Dundry Hill June 14, 1814 aged 32 years".

Go out the main entrance, passing on your left a 15th century building which is now used as Chew Magna's village hall.

It was originally a 'Church Ale House', but is known now as the 'Old Schoolroom', which reflects its use as a school from the 17th century.

SPOT CHECK

Can you find this object?

9. CHEW MAGNA

Chew Magna is the largest village in the district and was a thriving woollen centre in the Middle Ages. The manor of Chew was held by the Bishops of Bath and Wells from 1062 to 1548, and therefore was called Chew Episcopi or Bishop's Chew. Since about 1600, the name has been Chew Magna because this has been the most important of the several villages along the banks of the River Chew. The name 'Magna' comes from the Latin meaning 'the great'.

Opposite you on the High Street is the Bear and Swan pub. Next to it is the Pelican Inn (known as 'the Pelly') where you can enjoy a glass of Thatchers cider. Pass on your right the Moondance café and several shops. Continue along the raised pavement through the village for a few minutes, passing a number of beautiful old homes. Almost at the end and outside the opticians is a power pole with a footpath sign. This directs you across the road to the house called 'Staddle Stones' with staddle stones outside. Take the footpath down the side between stone walls. This leads you down to the River Chew again.

10. BRIDGE

Reach the medieval Tun Bridge with three pointed arches spanning 18m over the river. Cross and soon go over a much plainer, wooden footbridge.

A ***Stick racing.***

Turn right still following the Two Rivers Way.

11. RIVER

The path takes you into a field. Now it's simple. Take the right path, staying close to the river Chew. Sometimes you may be close to the river and at other times, a little removed.

A ***Make and sail a wooden boat.***

Cross footbridges and go through gates and eventually a footbridge ahead leads into woodland.

12. WOOD

Follow the path through the trees, over a footbridge and join a hard drive. Turn up left. Just before the gate at the top, turn right following the Two Rivers Way footpath sign in the field alongside the trees. The path at the end drops down to a kissing gate onto the road.

Cross the road back to the car park and café.

FACILITIES

The Pelican, tel: 01275 331777
The Bear and Swan, tel: 01275 331100
Salt & Malt, tel: 01275 333345

Glastonbury Market Cross - Chalice Well - Tor - Bushy Coombe - Market Cross

6.6km (4.1 miles) • Allow about 2.25 hours walking time
OS Explorer Map 141 • Cheddar Gorge & Mendip Hills West
Grid Ref: 498 389

Glastonbury is situated on the Isle of Avalon, within the Vale of Avalon. This ancient and somewhat mystical area has a history that goes back beyond the dawn of Christianity, made famous through the legend of King Arthur.

> ***Did you know?*** *The 'Isle of Avalon' means the 'Isle of the apple'.*

As you might well imagine, that possessing such a history, this area is still very much involved in the traditions of cider apple orcharding. Many varieties of cider apples have come from this area, including Dunkerton Sweet that was raised by the Dunkerton family in the village of Baltonsborough, close by. The family are still growing cider apples.

Fill your water bottle with fresh spring water bubbling out from Chalice Well at the start of this iconic Somerset walk, and go up and then down and around the other side of the Tor. It is brimming full of interest from the old market cross and fascinating Glastonbury High Street, to peaceful Chalice Well, the healing spring water, the wonderful Tor and its views, two very ancient oaks dating back to the birth of Christianity, and Tibetan prayer wheels.

A walk, with the steep climb up the Tor and down again. A good dog circle too.

Activities to enjoy:

- ***Take a water bottle to fill up with the fresh water from the White or Red Springs.***
- ***Magical sticky stones***
- ***Make a mini shelter***
- ***Make a grass whistle***

PARKING

In one of the main car parks in Glastonbury. To be safe, pay for four hours. St John's Pay and Display car park is a good choice on the site of the old station, near the High Street.

START

At the Market Cross at the bottom of the High Street. There is a choice of refreshment including several pubs that sell Thatchers

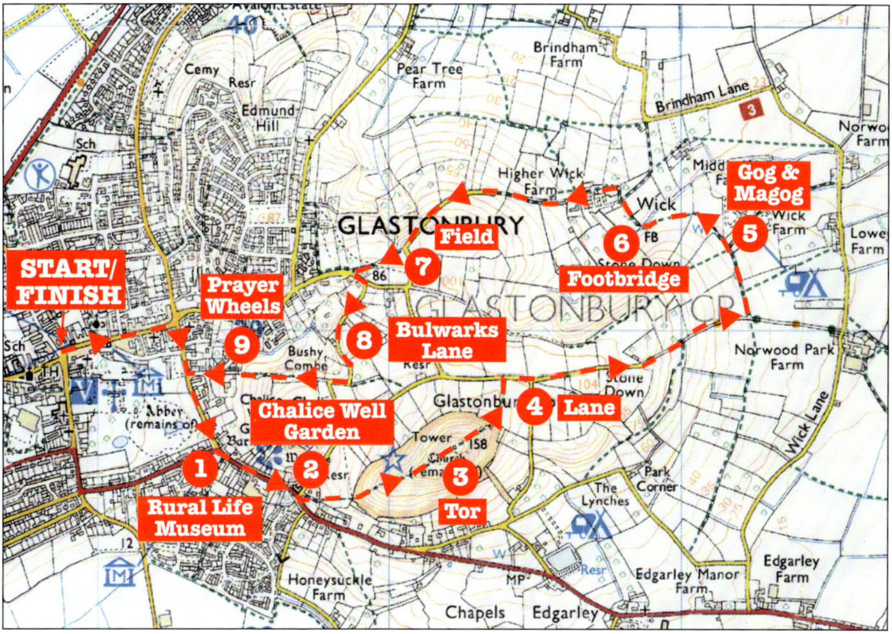

Cider. Walk up the High Street enjoying the sights, sounds and smells. Walk up one side and on the return, walk back down the other! Pass Glastonbury Tribunal, a 15th century building, probably once a merchant's house.

The Tribunal also houses the Glastonbury Lake Village Museum – which contains artefacts from one of Europe's most famous archaeological sites on the Somerset Levels near the town. Also pass St John's Church where a Holy Thorn thrives in the churchyard. This is said to come from a graft from the original thorn on Wearyall Hill nearby. It was thought to be 'miraculous' as it unusually flowered twice a year. The custom of sending a budded branch of the Holy Thorn to the Queen at Christmas which began during James I's reign, still carries on. The blossom comes from the tree in this churchyard.

At the top, with a Victorian drinking fountain opposite, turn right. Soon, over right is the wall to Glastonbury's beautiful old Abbey and Abbey grounds. Keep on, ignoring a footpath to the Tor.

1. RURAL LIFE MUSEUM

At the junction opposite is the Rural Life

Museum (getting a face lift and renovation in 2014/5) with an orchard on the corner. This reflects the many orchards that were in this area and around the Tor. Go along the raised pavement.

2. CHALICE WELL

Reach Chalice Well and gardens, a very special tranquil and spiritual place with a beautiful garden and a shop. The orchards have about 30 varieties of apple tree. The well is popular with all faiths, particularly pagans and in 2001 became a World Peace Garden. There is a charge for entry. Also here is one of the Holy Thorns of Glastonbury.

Continue past Chalice Well and turn left in Wellhouse Lane to visit the two healing springs where you can sample the water and fill up!

Here is the White Spring on the right which contains calcium or the one on the other side which is iron and red and comes down from the Chalice Well.

Return to the start of Wellhouse Lane and then turn up the public footpath which leads up the Tor.

Did you know? *There is a legend that says the Holy Grail is buried deep beneath the Tor, and that the red tainted water is the blood of Christ.*

3. TOR

It's worth looking at the Information Board about the Tor and also about the replanting of four apple orchards with traditional Somerset cider varieties, such as Kingston Black and Yarlington Mill

A ***Guess the number of steps to the top.***

On the way up look back at Wearyall Hill.

? ***Did you know?*** *Joseph of Arimathea was said to have landed at Wearyall Hill after the death of Christ, and planted his staff which grew to become the Holy Thorn. Wearyall Hill is the large 'whale back' feature seen to the South West of the Tor. Its name comes from 'weary all' after Joseph's long journey and eventual arrival.*

At the top come to St Michael's Tower. This is all that remains of the medieval chapel of St Michael, destroyed by earthquake in 1275.

It is a solemn occasion arriving here when one remembers the agonising death of the last Abbot of Glastonbury, Richard Whiting, and two others monks. It was the time of the Dissolution and they were imprisoned on trumped up charges and hung, drawn and quartered on the Tor in November 1539.

Enjoy all round views across Somerset. There's a toposcope here to help find the direction and distance, to notable landscape features in view.

A ***On a dry day the Tor is a great place to relax and look up at the sky to try a little Nephelococcygia – spotting shapes in the clouds.***

Facing the Tor as you came up, turn right down the steps which wind down the hill to the foot and then go along a path on the North East side of the Tor through Moneybox Field – so called because of the National Trust collection box here. To the right of the kissing gate on the right is the Millennium Stone which doubles up as a milestone.

4. LANE

Turn right on the lane (Stonedown Lane). At a junction, fork left on a smaller road which soon becomes a good hard track. Stay on this, ignoring side paths. Drop downhill and look for a large gateway on the left as the track levels out. Go through this gate and follow the trackway.

5. GOG AND MAGOG

Reach two ancient oaks on the right, named Gog and Magog by New Age people (see below). These two ancient Druid oaks probably about a thousand years old remain from a grove which once led up to the Tor by an ancient spring. They are often decorated with ribbons at pagan festivals.

After the trees, go through the wooden kissing gate on the right and follow the grassy track. A gate at the end leads into a field, now looking across to the Tor over left. Go diagonally down the field, cross a stile on the right, down steps and over a footbridge.

6. FOOTBRIDGE

Go up the field alongside a fence, cross a stile and continue ahead on a stony drive at the side of Higher Wick Farm which is run by the Paddington Trust. It provides holidays and educational breaks for groups, families or individuals. Pass close by a wattle and daub building on the left with sheep and clouds worked into the wall

Bend left passing the farm buildings and continue on the track/drive. Ignore any side paths. Glastonbury Tor is still in view as are the Mendip Hills. Climb very gently.

7. FIELD

On a corner, cross the stile ahead and go on in the field, staying over to the right edge. Go through a kissing gate and down a path to a lane. Follow it to the left.

8. BULWARKS LANE

Take the first turning right, Bulwarks Lane, a quiet, shady lane. Go round a very sharp right bend, and as the lane bends left, leave it and go straight on down a track. A kissing gate leads to a good viewpoint with

✓ SPOT CHECK

Can you find this object?

a seat. Down on the right is Bushy Coombe Nature Reserve. Go straight ahead and drop downhill to a gate and out to the end of a residential lane.

9. TIBETAN PRAYER WHEELS

Set in the wall of the holistic centre on the left are Tibetan Prayer Wheels, to be turned by passing pilgrims to send out their prayers into the world. Reach a junction with Abbey House opposite, where you were earlier.

Now turn right, retracing your steps. Turn back left down the High Street

Opposite Glastonbury Tribunal, just under an arch is a brass plaque *(right)* commemorating the hanging of six rebels of the Pitchfork Rebellion.

Yet another legend from this area of myth and magic involves the first Abbot of Glastonbury, St Dunstan. Dunstan is said to have made a pact with the Devil to wipe out the cider apple crop in the surrounding area, so that Dunstan could profit from beer that he intended to make from a good crop of grain. Well, the Devil kept his side of the bargain, (although Dunstan's side is somewhat uncertain) and sent a frost to kill the apple blossom in May.

The legend lives on, and today an air frost can come down through the Vale of Avalon in mid May and cause havoc with the open apple blossom. It's still called a 'Dunstan frost'.

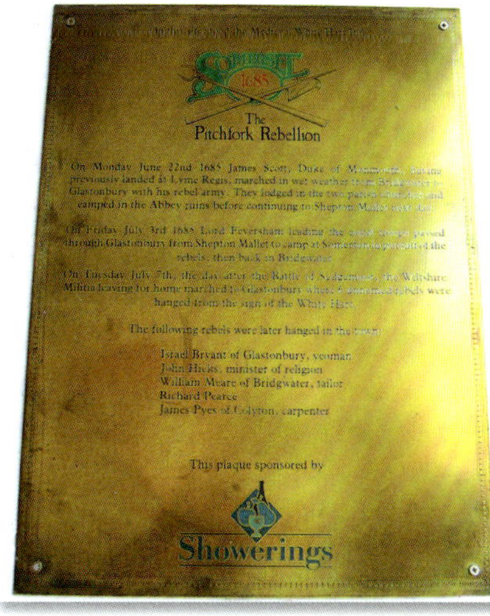

Maunsel Lock - Space Walk - Outwood - Coxhill bridge - Maunsel Lock

6km (3.7 miles) • Allow about 2 hours walking time
OS Explorer Map 140 • Quantock Hills & Bridgwater
Grid Ref: 307 297

In the heart of Somerset where apple growing and cider making has been flourishing for centuries, this circle is a walk 'in space'! It is a short circle south east of Bridgwater from near North Newton taking in planets on the Somerset Space Walk along the Bridgwater & Taunton Canal. Then circle back through the flat countryside on quiet lanes and paths to rejoin the canal towpath back to the start. Enjoy the wonderful canal side café where the walk starts. There is a good choice of picnic benches en route, too.

This part of the world lies at the very heart of Somerset and its cider traditions. When this canal was built there would have been very many more orchards seen from its towpath, and no doubt cider would have been drunk by those who worked and lived on the barges that carried the goods up and down this waterway. Today many of those orchards are gone, but apple trees still hold onto the landscape in gardens, small orchards and in the occasional hedgerow.

A Activities to enjoy:

• It could be good to make an apple flapjack before you go to have on one of the benches alongside the canal • Trail art • Grass whistle

PARKING

Canal side car park at Maunsel Lower Lock. Easily accessed from M5 J24, go through North Petherton and turn left to North Newton, crossing the motorway en route. Follow signs to Canal side car park (free parking). The centre, café and toilets are on the other side of the road here.

START

It's a good idea to read about the history of the canal on the board in the car park. This gives a good idea also of the work of volunteers to get this canal project up and running and of the importance to wildlife of this green and irrigated corridor.

Cross the canal bridge and turn right onto the towpath, immediately passing the last remaining lock-keeper's cottage.

A ***Anywhere along the canal towpath have a go at a little trail art, using all natural materials.***

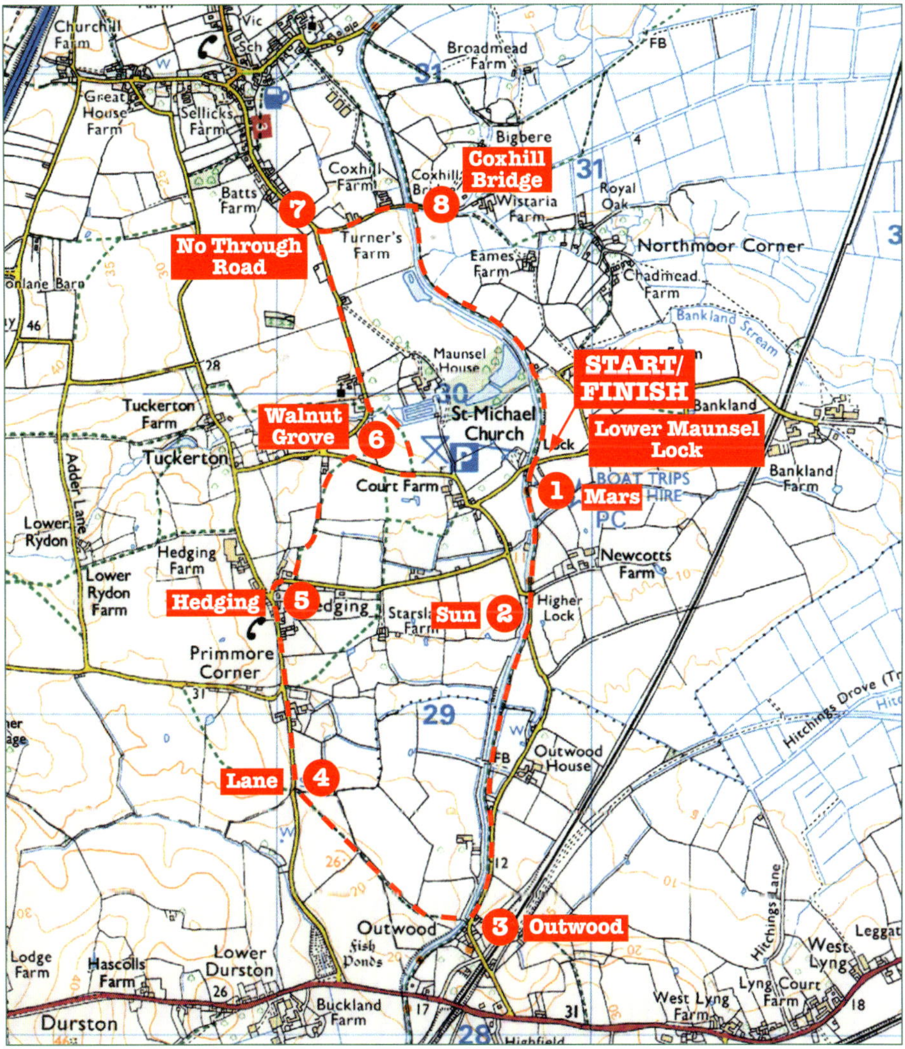

Soon reach the first of the planet model sculptures on this section of the Somerset Space Walk.

This is a sculpture trail model of the solar system, located along the 22.5km (14 mile) towpath from Bridgwater to Taunton. It was designed by Pip Youngman (who died in 2007) as a way of giving us an idea of the vastness of our own Solar System.

The models of the sun and planets are in proportionally correct sizes and distances apart. It is built to a scale of 1:530 million, so that 1mm equates to 530km.

The Sun is sited at Higher Maunsel Lock, further along, and one set of planets is installed in each direction along the canal. The Space Walk was opened in August 1997 by British astronomer Heather Couper.

1. MARS

The first planet is Mars, like the others, set in a round-top concrete plinth.

Continue to Earth. Can you spot the moon?

Then comes Venus and later Mercury.

Pass a private mooring on the other side of the canal and come up to Maunsel Higher Lock and the road.

2. THE SUN

On the other side of the bridge find the centre of the inner planets on this space walk, the Sun – a 2.5m (8'2") wide, 14-ton concrete sphere with a slice taken out to give two vertical faces upon which information is mounted.

Cross back to the side you were on and continue up the road for a few metres with the canal on your right.

Pass a pillbox on your left.

Did you know? *This type of concrete World War II defensive position became known as the 'pillbox' because of its shape. From inside, the defenders could fire through the slits in the side. Imagine standing guard here on a lonely night!*

Leave the road and rejoin the towpath with the canal still on your right.

You may pass fishermen along the route, and indeed if you look carefully you may see huge orange carp in the canal, and roach.

Pass another pillbox and keep on. Notice a couple of benches as you go along dedicated to local foster parents who took in evacuee children during the last war.

Carry on all the way to another footbridge at Outwood.

3. OUTWOOD

Cross the canal here and take the marked stile on the left across a rough field. Go diagonally up across the field passing a power pole on your left, and then a pond on your right and go through a gap in the hedge. Turn right along the hedge. In the corner continue along a broad grassy track between hedges leading to another field.

A ***Have a go at making and using a grass whistle.***

Then keep right beside the hedge through the field which brings you out onto a lane.

In the field you may be able to spot a four leaf clover.

? ***Did you know?*** *Clover is an amazing plant that can capture nitrogen from air that we breathe and store it in nodules or tiny lumps on its root system. When the plant is cut down or grazed by animals, it releases this nitrogen into the soil to help it re-grow. Peas and beans do the same in your garden.*

4. LANE

Follow this to the right, soon coming to a small hamlet of Primmore (not named) and then on to Hedging.

5. HEDGING

Turn right on the small lane, go round a corner and after passing two houses on the left, cross left over a stile on the marked footpath. Follow the left hedge round two corners and pass a power pole and then go straight on through a gap into the next field. Continue along the hedge and cross a stile near the corner into another field. Keep more or less straight across. When you reach a rough area ahead, go right and then left in the same direction as before. When you reach the hedge ahead of you, go out through the large metal gate on your left out onto the lane. Turn right and after a few minutes cross left over a stile into a grove of walnuts.

6. WALNUT GROVE

Parallel the right edge and then head across to a large farmhouse on the far side going between the trees. Over on your left on the edge, notice a ha-ha.

Did you know? *A 'ha-ha' was a feature used by country houses to stop grazing animals getting into the garden from the surrounding parkland. The great country house owners didn't want ugly fences ruining the view, so they had a trench dug. Those who approached this feature were to look in amazement at its sudden appearance and utter the words 'ha-ha' in surprise.*

Take the large wooden gate ahead and then go left out by the mill house to a lane. Turn right, rising very gently. At the top, notice a drive on the left which leads to St Michael's church, a very picturesque small church, which probably won't be open. But it is worth looking at it and noticing the well clipped yews each side of the path to the front entrance. It's a very pretty, candle-lit Saxon chapel on the estate of Maunsel House and is often used for weddings by guests at the house.

SPOT CHECK

Can you find this object?

Continue on the road. Pass the entrance to Maunsel House on your right – a magnificent 14th century manor, now a popular wedding venue.

7. NO THROUGH ROAD

Take the No Through Road on the right and after a few minutes reach the canal again at Coxhill Bridge.

8. COXHILL BRIDGE

Go down left through a gate and left back under the bridge. Notice the black iron clad corners on the bridge on the left, with grooves made by the ropes of the barges being pulled along the canal. The second one has the most grooves. Follow the canal on your right. Soon pass a beautiful line of poplars on the other side and go under power lines, decked out with balls, to prevent swans from crashing into the lines.

Come back to the bridge at Lower Maunsel and the end of this circle.

1. How to make a grass whistle

This is great fun, and so easy! Find a wide blade of grass. Hold your hands together with your thumbs pointing back towards you and your fingers in the air, much like you would for a prayer. Trap the blade of grass between your thumbs , and the fleshy part at the base of your thumbs. Make sure it's taut, and blow hard on the leaf edge which is held tight between your thumbs. With a little practice you can make an interesting noise, and it is different every time!

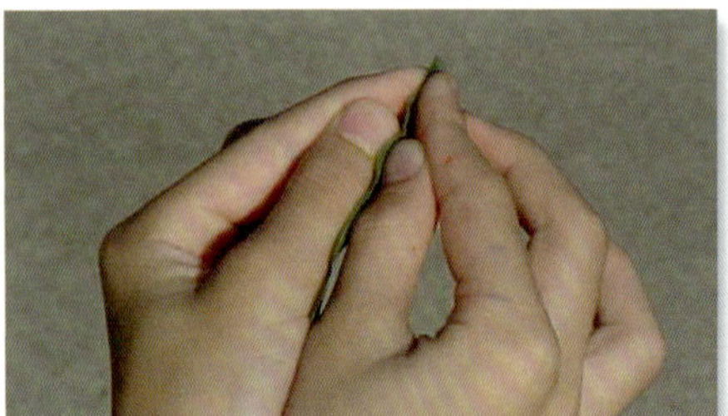

2. Sticky stones

This is a bit of fun! Find three stones of about 25-30cm across. Ask your friend or parent to press two of them together hard for the count of 30 using mainly the tips of fingers. It can be tiring!

Meanwhile you take the other stone and make small circles around their hands almost like the moon orbiting the planet.

It needs to be up and down, not side to side, and maybe you say a few 'magic words'.

At the end ask the person to gently try and prise the stones apart. They should find it quite hard, as though the stones are held together by some special force.

3. Trail Art

Trail Art is simple and fun. Use the natural materials you pass on the trail – sticks, leaves etc. – to make a picture or a sculpture that you can leave behind.

The only rules are, as for mini-shelter building, that you don't damage any living plants or trees. And don't use plastic, metal or non-biodegradable string. Everything must be natural.

Here are some examples of trail art that we made. We expect you can do much better!

4. How to find the age of a tree

Bring string, and a ruler or tape measure. You need two people for this. First of all measure from the base of the tree 1.5m up, and get your helper to mark the spot. Next run the string around the outside of the tree trunk, but try to avoid a spot where there are bulges or lumps. You have now measured the circumference of the tree, which you will need to divide by 2.5cm. This means that for every 2.5cm your tree is one year old. Although this is not completely accurate it will give you a rough idea of the tree's age. By counting backwards you can work out the date when it started to grow.

There is another way of finding out how old a tree is. Simply count the number of annual rings on the cut end of the trunk.

What was happening in history at that time?

5. Compass in a puddle

Here is a very simple compass that you can easily make and use in a puddle or cup of water. You will need:

- A paper clip
- Magnet (a fridge magnet will do)
- Leaf

First undo the paper clip until you have just the small loop at the end, you can use this as a handle later. Next magnetise the opened end of the paper clip by rubbing the magnet down it in one direction. Once it has been magnetised, thread it through your leaf down the centre rib, and gently place it on the water. Watch as it turns the magnetised end of the paper clip towards north.

6. Shapes and faces in the trees and rocks

Using your imagination, look carefully and see if you can see faces of animals or mythical creatures in the trees and rocks as you follow the trails. Here are some that we found.

Elephant

Pig

7. Spotting shapes in clouds... or Nephelococcygia

It's a fun way to relax and enjoy the glorious clouds in the wide blue yonder above us. Do you know there is even a Cloud Appreciation Society... take a look at their website for some amazing cloud shapes. The Society was founded by Gavin Pretor-Pinney from Britain in January 2005 and aims to foster understanding and appreciation of clouds. At November 2013 it had over 35,000 members worldwide from 165 different countries.

Yahoo named the society's website as "the most weird and wonderful find on the internet for 2005".

8. Mini shelter building

Could you survive if you were 10cm tall?

This is all about design and building that is only limited by your imagination!

Building a mini shelter to house 'very tiny people' is great fun, and you don't need any experience.

Collect plenty of dead sticks and find a suitable area, perhaps in woodland or a clearing, and let your imagination do the rest! Or make a stone shelter by collecting different pebbles and stones and combine sticks or feathers or seaweed – whatever is there to use.

The only rule is don't pick or break off any living plants or branches. Only use dead or fallen sticks. Leave your shelter when it is finished. You never know what small creatures may use your little house!

9. Leaf rubbing

You will need:

At home: Some plain white thin paper, a wax crayon

On the walk: Take a book and some kitchen roll so you can keep the leaf flat until you get home.

Choose a leaf with fairly pronounced veins on the back. We chose a cob nut leaf. Oak is good, and beech and also wych elm. Try a few and see how you get on.

When you get home, put the leaf flat on a hard surface and lay the sheet of paper on top. Press down gently, so the leaf is flat and you can just start to see the shape underneath. Hold it firmly and with the wax crayon rub gently over the leaf, trying not to go over the edges. Try different techniques – rubbing in one direction and keeping an even pressure is good. Don't push the tip of the crayon into the paper. You will find the best way with practice.

Then, hey presto! You have your leaf as a record. Write down the name of the leaf and on which walk you found it.

10. Making and sailing a boat

Why not try and make your own boat – whether a sailing boat or a raft, or whatever – and see if it will float. Here is one we made and sailed on the pond. As always, the only rules are that you don't damage any living trees or plants, and don't use any materials that won't break down naturally.

11. Jacks

The game is also known by other names such as *Fivestones*, *Chuckstones*, *Dibs*, *Dabs*, *Tally* and *Knucklebones*.

Jacks: All you need is five small stones (no bigger than 1.5cm across) and a small cleared area. It can be played on the ground with players kneeling, or played on a bench or table so you can stand.

The Play: The first player throws five stones into the air with one hand and tries to catch as many as possible on the back of the same hand.

The stones that are caught are thrown up again from the back of the hand and as many as possible are caught in the palm of the same hand. If no stones end up being caught, your turn is over.

One by one: If you did catch one or more stones then you can carry on. Keep one of the caught stones in the same hand and throw the others down gently. Now throw the single stone into the air, and at the same time try to pick up one of the stones on the ground and then catch the stone you threw up – all with the same hand. Keep going and do this again until all the stones have been picked up one by one.

Throw down four of the stones again, throw the single stone in the air, and try to pick up two stones with the same hand before catching the tossed stone. This is repeated again with two stones and then at the end toss and pick up the remaining one stone.

Do this again for three stones – picking them up together while tossing a stone in the air.

Finally, all four stones are picked up together before catching the single tossed stone.

If you drop the thrown stone your turn is over.

When the stones are too spread out to pick them up together, you can throw the stone in the air as usual but then try to knock the stones together into a group and then catch the stone again, of course!

Once the stones are grouped together you can try picking them up in twos, threes or fours, depending where you are in the game.

The player loses his go when he doesn't catch the stone. The first one to complete the game wins.

11. Thatchers Apple Flapjack Energy Bars

These sweet, sticky treats are the perfect mid walk pick-me-up. Full of fast release carbs from the sugar, backed up with slow release carbs from the oats and bursting with appley goodness and rich oats and honey, they are sure to encourage even the most reluctant of walkers to greater things.

Making these is a walk in the park *(sorry)* and with such a simple recipe there is minimal faffing to get to the good stuff, just simply, weigh, melt, mix and bake and away you go.

You will need:

- A 25 x 25 cm baking tin at least 2 cm deep or equivalent oblong one, well buttered and lined with non-stick bakers parchment
- A medium sized saucepan
- A pre-heated fan oven, 165° C

Ingredients :

- 225g salted organic butter
- 200g unrefined brown organic sugar
- 150g local honey, set or runny are both fine
- 250g jumbo porridge oats
- 200g pinhead oatmeal
- 3 apples, grated, skin on, cores discarded
- ¼ teaspoon all spice powder
- the zest and juice of one lemon

Method:

Set the butter, sugar and honey to melt slowly on the stove.

Finely grate the zest of the lemon and place in a small mixing bowl. Add the juice from the same lemon. Grate the apples and add to the lemon, mix well.

Add the allspice to the melted ingredients and stir in the apple and lemon mix.

Lastly, add the oats and the oatmeal and mix thoroughly.

Place this mix in the baking tray and pat down firmly with the back of a spatula.

Bake for 20 minutes or until lightly golden.

Remove from the oven and allow to cool a little before cutting into squares or bars. Once properly cooled they can be lifted out of the tray and stored until needed.

You may find that they mysteriously disappear before the intended walk, so a guard should be posted to keep an eye on the tin...